EVOLUTION

EVOLUTION

A PRESUMPTUOUS THEORY

Jo Schermerhorn-Rorex

and

Evelyn Cole-Stuck

Library of Congress Control Number: 2009906048
ISBN: Hardcover   978-1-4415-4712-5
                    Softcover   978-1-4415-4711-8

This book was printed in the United States of America.

To order additional copies of this book, contact:
Xlibris Corporation
1-888-795-4274
www.Xlibris.com
Orders@Xlibris.com
62100

CONTENTS

We dedicate this book to our mother, Josephine. She was a very courageous lady who, although handicapped and in much pain, her spirit always made us all feel better just by being in the room with her. She was always there for us.

Thank you, Mom.

presume: suppose, assume, surmise
          conjecture, guess

theory: speculation, supposition, premise
          conjecture, hypothesis

by: Jo Schermerhorn-Rorex and
Evelyn Cole-Stuck

FOREWORD

So, you may ask, "What do an Emergency Room nurse and a Senior Hospital Medical Transcriber know?" That is totally immaterial. Every scientific fact known to mankind is available at the touch of a button.—Turn on your computer. Welcome to the Internet!

The education, training, and work experience of both of us has been in the medical field, so we will base our discourse on modern medical knowledge, and on 21st Century scientific studies of the human body, stem cell research, DNA, and genetic coding.

EVOLUTION—
A PRESUMPTUOUS THEORY

The "beginning" is not a lifeless "soup", in a lifeless ocean, on a lifeless planet, in a lifeless solar system, in a possible lifeless galaxy.

The "beginning" is a space, atoms, gravity, magnetic forces, and the origin of the exact and complex formulas for atmosphere (78% nitrogen, 21% oxygen, and 1% carbon dioxide and other gases), for water (H_2O, 2 parts hydrogen to 1 part oxygen), the formulas for the 106 known elements, and the even more complex formulas for the 20 amino acids which form protein.

Protoplasm is the base of all life—plant and animal—and protoplasm is formed of protein, fats and carbohydrates.

Evolution theorists make no effort to explain these origins. They just presume that lifeless matter in a lifeless "soup" was struck by some unknown force and suddenly sprang to life by some unknown process, and evolved in to all the life forms that have ever existed on planet earth—plant and animal.

Not one shred of evidence has ever been discovered to validate their theory—no sediment in ancient soil or rocks of any pre-biotic "soup"; no parts or parts of parts of any organism or plant evolving in to a different species.

To date, the "beginning" remains an unsolved mystery.

OTHER THEORIES

Evolution is not the only theory being presented in the 21st Century. We will discuss only briefly the theories of Panspermia, the Big Bang, and Intelligent Design. We will not address the Biblical Story of Creation. We will discuss Evolution in detail.

PANSPERMIA:

Proponents of the Panspermia theory tell us that life originated "somewhere" in space and "floated" to Earth, which doesn't answer the question of how life originated. How did it originate in space?

They completely ignore the extreme hazards of space travel—the extreme heat, cold, radiation, lack of oxygen, collision with space debris, and the attraction of gravity towards other planets in passing.

Scientists have been unable to detect signs of life in our solar system. The nearest planet to Earth outside our solar system, which may or may not support life, is 10.5 light years away. That's 63 trillion miles.

What does the Panspermia theory offer to prove how, why, when and where life originated? Nothing.

THE BIG BANG:

Proponents of the Big Bang theory presume that the Universe was hanging somewhere in space. They do not explain how space or the Universe originated. Somewhere in space there was a mass of unspecified size—just hanging there for some unknown reason.

Gravity supposedly came later as it is not mentioned by the Big Bang theorists. They do not explain space, or what part of space the Universe occupied, or what part of the Universe the mass occupied. Nor what mysterious force caused the mass to explode, and the billions of galaxies, stars, and the planets all burst out of this mass, and reached their present locations.

Theorists report the temperature a million years after the "Big Bang" to be 5000°F. That would have eradicated all life forms we know of on earth.

What does the Big Bang theory offer to prove how, why, when and where life originated? Nothing.

INTELLIGENT DESIGN:

Some theorists, who did not accept the evolution theory because the awesome complexities of the brain, eyes, the kidneys, lungs, liver, etc., caused them to acknowledge that more than evolution's "blind random chance," was required to develop the process by which these marvelous structures were formed, advanced the "Intelligent Design" theory.

These proponents accept the idea of intelligent design. Do they know the name of the Intelligent Designer?

EVOLUTION:

Evolution theorists begin with the presumption that life originated in a lifeless "soup," in a lifeless ocean, on a lifeless planet, in a lifeless solar system—in possibly a lifeless galaxy—when some unknown force struck a bit of lifeless matter, which suddenly sprang to life. This bit of unknown matter, presumably by "blind random chance" and a hit and miss process Darwin called "natural selection" and "survival of the fittest", with the aid of only beneficial mutations, evolved into all the creatures in the sea, from sponges and coral to giant squids and whales; into all the creatures on land, from bacteria to elephants and giraffes, including mankind; and all the creatures with wings, including penguins, bats and ostriches.

They presume all this occurred, although, modern scientists acknowledge that for every beneficial mutation, a thousand or more harmful or lethal mutations occur, which result in freaks and monstrosities.

Although, this "soup" is basic to such a concept of evolution, and the origin of life, it is only a presumption. There is not one shred of evidence that any such "soup" ever existed, nor that a mysterious force caused a lifeless element to suddenly spring to life in such a "soup."

In ancient rocks, some estimated as being 3500 to 3900 million years old, no where on the Earth, despite all the searching, has any speck of a sediment of this remarkable "soup" been found, and not one small piece of any fossil of any life form evolving or partly evolving into another life form.

Theorists have just arranged their suppositions to fit and support their presumptions.

Although evolution theorists are still adamantly promoting and defending their theory, even Charles Darwin had his doubts. He wrote to Asa Gray, a botanist, "imagination must fill in the very wide gaps."

Darwin and others explained these "gaps" by citing "an incomplete fossil record" or "they just haven't been discovered yet."

The "gaps" remain today.

Evolution's Unsolved Mysteries

A presumed "soup" is not the beginning. Earth is not the beginning. The presumption of a "soup" or "slime" does not answer the questions of how our magnificent Universe originated, nor how space originated, nor how expansive is space, nor what may be in space beyond the reach of modern telescopes. Presumptions are not fact or science. Scientific conclusions need to be observed, examined, and duplicated to be validated.

Evolution theorists make no effort to explain the following mysteries.

1. Explain space. Where does it begin? Where does it end?
2. How did the Universe originate?
3. How did the billions of galaxies originate?
4. How did the stars (suns) originate?
5. How did the solar systems originate?
6. How did the planets form?
7. What determined their location in Space?
8. Where did the force of gravity that holds everything in place originate? What actually is gravity?
9. How did the exact formula for the atmosphere (78% nitrogen, 21% oxygen, and 1% carbon dioxide and other gases) originate?
10. How did the exact formula for water (2 parts hydrogen, 1 part oxygen) originate? For salt water add sodium chloride.

11. How did soil form?
12. How did the oceans form?
13. How, why, when, and where did over a hundred different chemical elements form?
14. How did the exact complex formulas for the 20 amino acids, essential to all life—plant and animal—form?

It requires 20 specific amino acids to form a protein, that with lipids (fats) and carbohydrates (starches and sugars), forms protoplasm, which is the basis for all life forms—plant and animal—that have ever existed on Earth.

The exact formula of specific elements had to join together in each amino acid, and float together in the "soup," and join with the other 19 amino acids, and remain together, keeping all other elements out—presumably in a "soup" that was moving about.

Formulas—Chemical Elements & Amino Acids

There are 106 known elements on Earth. Many are essential to life on Earth—plant and animal. (H^2O) 2 parts hydrogen to 1 part oxygen is the exact formula for water. 78% nitrogen, 21% oxygen and 1% carbon dioxide and other gases is the exact formula for our atmosphere. Evolutionists tell us these elements "floated" down from "somewhere." From where? How did they form there?

actinium—Ac
aluminum—Al
americium—Am
antimony—Sb
argon—Ar
arsemic—As
astatine—At
barium—Ba
berketrium—Bk
berre;;ium—Be
bismuth—Bi
boron—B
bromine—Br
cadmium—Cd
calcium Ca

californium—Cf
carbon—C
cerium—Cr
cesium—Cs
chlorine—Cl
chromium—Cr
cobalt—Co
copper—Cu
curium—Cm
dysprosium—Dy
einsteinium—Es
element 106
erbium—Er
europium—Eu
fermium—Fm

fluorine—F
francium—Fr
gadolinium—Gd
gallium—Ga
germanium—Ge
gold—Au
Hafnium—Hf
helium—He
hahnium—Ha
helium—He
holmium—Ho
hydrogen—H
indium—In
iodine—I
iridium—Ir
iron—Fe
krypton—Kr
lanthanum—La
lawrencium—Lr
lead—Pb
lithium—Li
lutetium—Lu
magnesium—Mg
manganese—Mn
mendelevium—Md
mercury—Hg
molybedenum—Mo
neodumium—Nd
neon—Ne
neptunium—Np
nickel—Ni
niobium—Nb
nitrogen—N
nobelium—No
osmium—Os
oxygen O
palladium—Pd
phosphorus—P

platinum—Pt
plutonium—Pu
polonium—Po
potassium—K
praseodymium—Pr
promethium—Pm
protactinium—Pa
radium Ra
radon—Rn
rhenium—Rs
rhodium—Rh
rubidium—Rb
ruthenium—Ru
rutherfordium Rf
samarium—Sm
scandium—Sc
selenium—Se
silicon—Si
silver—Ag
sodium—Na
strontium—Sr
sulfur—S
tantalum—Ta
technetium—Tc
tellurium—Te
terbium—Tb
thallium—Tl
tin—Sn
titanium—Ti
tungsten—W
uranium—U
vanadium—V
xenon—Xe
Ytterbium—Yb
Yttrium—Y
zinc—Zn
zirconium Zr

Protoplasm is basic for all life on earth—plant and animal. Protoplasm is formed from fats, carbohydrates, and proteins. About 2000 proteins are needed for cellular activity in the body.

20 separate amino acids are essential to form protein. Each amino acid is a very complex formula of four of the 106 known elements. What formed these exact formulas? How did the exact amounts of *some* of the 106 elements join, keeping out all the 102, in a supposedly moving about "soup," until some mysterious force struck them and lifeless matter suddenly sprang to life?

There are over 100 elements, but only four are present in the amino acids (C, H, N, O) which form proteins

alamine	$C_3H_7NO^2_2$
arginine	$C_6H_{14}N_4O_2$
asparagine	$C_4H_8N_2O_3$
aspartic acid	$C_4H_7NO_4$
cysteine	$C_3H_7NO_2S$
glutamic acid	$C_5H_9NO_4$
glutamine	$C_5H_{10}N_2O_3$
glycine	$C_2H_5NO_2$
histidine	$C_6H_9N_3O_2$
isoleucine	$C_6H_{13}NO_2$
leucine	$C_6H_{13}NO_2$
lysine	$C_6H_{14}N_2O_2$
methionine	$C_5H_{11}NO_2S$
phenylalanine	$C_9H_{11}NO_2$
proline	$C_5H_9O_2N$
serine	$C_3H_7NO_3$
threonine	$C_4H_9NO_3$
tryptophan	$C_{11}H_{12}N_2O_2$
tyrosine	$C_9H_{13}NO^3$
valine	$C_5H_{11}NO^2$

Protein is an extremely complex combination of 20 amino acids, and is a basic component of all plant and animal matter. Protein contains the elements carbon, hydrogen, nitrogen, oxygen, sometimes sulfur, phosphorus, iron and iodine. It also includes essential compounds such as enzymes, hormones, and immunoglobins.

Is it believable that the exact, complex formulas for all 20 amino acids accidently originated at the same time, in the same place, remained together, keeping out all other elements and formed a protein.

Proteins are extremely complex. Some proteins are structural and some are enzymes. Protein enzymes are needed for cellular activity.

What are the odds of even a single protein forming by "blind random chance" in a lifeless "soup"?

It has been estimated, and evolutionists acknowledge, that the chances are only 1 in 10^{113}—that's 1 followed by 113 zeros.

100,000,000,000,000,000,000,000,000,000,000,000,000,000,00 0,000,000,000,000,000,000,000,000,000,000,000,000,000,000, 000,000,000,000,000,000

How did the chemical elements drift into a "soup" that could not exist without some of the elements already being present?

This "soup" had to be liquid. The exact formula for water is two parts hydrogen and one part oxygen. For salt water add sodium chloride.

How did life originate in this lifeless "soup?"

Theorists claim chemical elements by some unknown process formed the 20 amino acids. The 20 amino acids are necessary for life as we know it to exist.

What was the lifeless matter that mysteriously sprang to life? It had to be protoplasm. Protoplasm is the only known form of matter in which life is manifested, both plant and animal.

Protoplasm is a formula of lipids (fats), carbohydrates (sugars and starches), proteins, and inorganic salts.

The Beginning

In the beginning . . . .
Such a simple phrase with so many interpretations.
In the beginning was space.
Was it empty space? Absolutely not!

SPACE: The continuous boundless expanse, extending in all dimensions
and directions, of unknown size or time of origin—infinite.

After space, atoms, matter, the 106 known elements had to appear
from somewhere.

ATOMS: Atoms are the building blocks of all matter—organic and
inorganic. What distinguishes one thing from another is the
number of protons and neutrons in the nucleus, and the number
and arrangement of the electrons revolving around it. Protons
carry a positive charge, neutrons carry no charge, and electrons
circle the nucleus and carry a negative charge.

An atomic bomb, exploded, can destroy a city, but what mysterious
force holds all the atoms in the Universe together?

MATTER: Anything that takes up space. All matter is made up of atoms.

All matter, whether a human, an animal, a plant or a piece of
furniture can be arranged in an exact sequence by the number of

atoms present. Science has not explained the how, why, where, or when each exact sequence originated.

ELEMENTS: There are over a hundred known elements. Combinations of these elements form our atmosphere, water, amino acids, etc. Our atmosphere is 78% nitrogen, 21% oxygen, and 1% carbon dioxide and other gasses. Water is 2 parts hydrogen to one part oxygen. How these combinations formed originally and remain the same today is not explained by science, but different combinations might have resulted in air poisonous to breathe and water poisonous to drink,

The gases and dust which scientists say formed the entire universe derive from these elements.

Evolutionists vaguely explain these elements "floated" down to Earth. Where did they "float" from? Where did they originate?

How could "blind random chance" form any specific matter from these 106 known elements?

GRAVITY: Mysterious force that holds everything in place. How, why, when and where it originated is unexplained.

Gravity keeps the Earth's heat from escaping into space. Atmosphere is held in place by gravity—just the right force to keep the earth's atmosphere from escaping into space, the right force to keep us bound to Earth, but not too much force to keep us from moving about.

THE UNIVERSE

How, why, when and where did the Universe originate?

Researchers have estimated the age of the Universe to be between 11.2 and 20 billion years.

They have based their estimations on the presumed age of chemical elements, the presumed age of the presumed oldest stars, and the presumed ages of white dwarf stars.

Scientists have concluded our universe was formed from gases and dust, so gases and dust had to exist in space when the universe was formed. But for how, why, when, and where these gases and dust originated, scientists have no answer.

As far as the strongest telescope can reach, observers can see billions of stars, but what is further out in space, is yet to be revealed. Some scientists have speculated there may be more than one universe.

The size of the Universe cannot be estimated.

The Universe can be observed only as far as the strongest telescope reaches.

The Universe is governed by certain well-developed uniform laws. Can this constancy have been reached instantly by "blind random chance? Did all those galaxies in the Universe just bang around for a few millenniums until they reached their present locations?

The majesty and orderliness of the Universe is astounding. The timing of movements is constant, century after century, year after year, month after month, day after day.

The precision is so constant, we can set our watches by it.

If we look up at the awesome, majestic panorama in the night sky, can we believe it is the result of "blind random chance?" Can we believe scientists have it all figured out? What mysterious force holds all this in perfect order? Scientists have named this force gravity, but they cannot explain what gravity is or where it originated.

GALAXIES: A galaxy is a vast group of stars.

Some astronomers estimate there are billions of galaxies in the universe. Each galaxy may contain hundreds of billions of stars (suns).

About 10 billion galaxies can be seen in the Universe with modern telescopes.

Galaxies do not hang helter skelter in space but are in clusters.

Some clusters contain a few galaxies, and many are made up of hundreds, possibly thousands, or more, of galaxies.

Astronomers have photographed thousands of these galactic clusters. Our Milky Way is part of a cluster of approximately 20 galaxies.

OUR GALAXY—THE MILKY WAY:

Until 1924, the MW was the only known galaxy until Edwin Hubble (1889-1953), an astronomer, demonstrated there were several other galaxies observable in the sky.

But our galaxy is only a speck of what is in space. About ten billion are in the observable part of the universe. There are many more beyond the range of our modern telescopes.

The MW is about 600 quadrillion miles in diameter. At the speed of light (186,282 miles a second) it would take 100 thousand years to cross from one side to the other.

Our solar system revolves around the Galaxy at approximately half a million miles an hour. At that speed it would take 200 million years to revolve one time. Consider the speed of light—186,232 miles a second. At that speed, light could circle the Earth 7 and a half times in a second.

The average distance between stars (suns) in the Milky Way is estimated to be about six light years. That's about 36 trillion miles.

The Milky Way is a vast group of stars. Astronomers have estimated there are over a billion. Others have estimated from 200 to 400 billions. Our solar system is just a speck in this Galaxy, which is considered to be 90,000 light years across.

Astronomers now believe solar systems are common in the Universe. and that half the stars (suns) in the Universe have planets orbiting them, and possibly some of the planets are similar to Earth.

The sun, moon, and nine planets comprise our solar system. Planets named in order to their closeness to the sun are Mercury, Venus, Earth, Mars, Jupiter, Saturn, Uranus, Neptune and Pluto. An estimated 100,000 asteroids and a hundred billion comets, as well as meteors, are involved. All but three planets have their own moons orbiting them.

Scientists estimate our solar system formed about four and a half billion years ago.

Recently scientists have questioned if Pluto is a planet.

THE SUN

The Sun appears as a gaseous sphere.

It's the star at the center of our solar system. The sun is about 865,000 miles in diameter, 93 million miles from Earth.

Its source of energy is nuclear fusion reactions.

The sun is the star around which the Earth and other planets revolve. It provides light, heat and energy.

Light from the sun takes about 8 minutes to reach the Earth.

THE MOON

The moon is a satellite of Earth, 2160 miles in diameter. It takes 27,332 days to orbit the Earth.

As it orbits it rotates on its axis so the moon always presents the same side toward Earth.

It reflects light from the sun and its phases are the result of increased or decreased areas of its surface reflecting sunlight.

The new moon occurs when the moon is turned away from the sun. The full moon occurs when the moon's entire surface is illuminated by the sun.

The moon is about 239,000 miles from Earth, and is about one-fourth the size of Earth.

The moon has no atmosphere, but in 1972 the Apollo mission reported possible traces of water.

On July 20, 1969, the first man landed on the moon.

EARTH

Earth is the only planet in our solar system known to support life.

According to scientists Earth suffered many catastrophes to form its crust, shape its sea beds and mountains, and move continents.

Scientists presume that Earth is four and a half billion years old, hanging there in space, 93,000,000 miles from the sun, the exact distance to establish the earth's temperature to sustain life as we know it.

The earth orbits the sun at a speed of 66,600 miles an hour, just the right speed to off-set the pull of gravity toward the sun. If the speed decreased the earth would move further from the sun and become too cold. If the speed increased earth would move closer to the sun and become too hot. The earth orbits the sun once a year. The earth rotates on its axis every 24 hours, establishing day and night. As it rotates, the earth tilts at 23.5 degrees which brings about the seasons. The earth is 7927 miles in diameter.

The Earth's orbit is third from the sun. Earth is the fifth largest planet in our solar system.

What does Earth have that other planets in our solar system do not?

There had to be an ozone layer, atmosphere, water, and elements.

The ozonosphere extends from about 6 miles to about 30 miles above Earth, and protects from ultraviolet radiation and helps protect Earth from heat loss,

Atmosphere is the gaseous envelope (air) surrounding the earth. It is 78% nitrogen, 21% oxygen, 1% carbon dioxide and other gases. This is exactly the right formula essential to sustain all the life forms we know of on Earth.

It extends to a height of about 22,000 miles above the Earth. It rotates with the Earth

Less than one percent of the atmosphere is carbon dioxide. Without carbon dioxide plants would die. Plants take in carbon dioxide and exude oxygen. Animals breathe in oxygen and breathe out carbon dioxide. Without this exchange neither species could survive. Amazing.

Atmosphere protects the Earth from ultra violet rays, and from meteors striking the earth. Meteors burn up entering the atmosphere.

Atmosphere also contributes to the changing colors in the sky. Astronauts returning from space travel marvel at the beauty of our Earth.

WATER

The Earth has vast amounts of water. The exact formula for water is H^2O.

Isn't it fortunate, that this formula evolved by "blind random chance?" Isn't it fortunate that rain comes down in drops, snow comes down in flakes, and ice comes down in pellets, not in great blobs? Water can be vapor, snow, or ice, but it remains $H2O$.

Evolution theorists would have us believe that by "blind random chance" oceans just happened to form. They ignore water is formed by two parts hydrogen and one part oxygen. Any other combination and it would not be water. Add another element and it might be toxic. it might kill all organisms.

Every second the sun's heat changes millions of gallons of water into vapor, which is lighter than air. Vapor forms into clouds, which are moved by wind and air currents, and falls as rain in other areas.

During lightning storms oxygen combines with nitrogen and the compounds are delivered to the soil and plants absorb them as fertilizer.

SOIL

Soil contains the elements essential for plants. The soil also contains elements for humans and animal life after vegetation converts these elements into forms that a body can assimilate.

Many millions of various microscopic organisms can be found in a handful of soil, and these tiny organisms work to convert dead leaves, grass, and waste matter, to loosen the soil so water and air can get in. Some bacteria convert this into compounds that plants need for growth, Worms and insects improve topsoil by bringing subsoil to the surface.

Even soil that has been misused, or where fire or volcanoes have caused damage, or pollution has damaged the soil, it can repair the damage and again the land can be restored.

All debris returns to soil "From dust thou are to dust returneth."

EVOLUTION

The evolution theory did not originate with Charles Darwin.

Early Norse mythology depicted Ymir (a giant), and Andumla (a cow) were formed as warm winds melted snow.

Anaximander (611-547 BC) a Greek naturalist, philosopher, surmised that life developed in "sea slime."

Empedocles (490-430 BC) a Greek philosopher, poet and statesman, surmised that as a result of the flow of matter, fantastic shapes and objects were formed by chance—heads without bodies, eyes without faces, arms and legs would sometimes accidently join to create monsters; such as animal heads with human bodies, and human heads with animal bodies.

David Hume (1711-1776) philosopher, economist, and historian, proposed that the world was composed of particles of matter that were in perpetual motion and after a significant period of time these particles might form any combination and this random motion could eventually create conformations that could survive.

Evolution theorists presume that all life began in a lifeless "soup" in a lifeless ocean, on a lifeless planet, in a lifeless solar system. by "blind random chance" and a hit and miss process Darwin called "natural selection". and "survival of the fittest," when some unknown force (possibly lightning) connected with some unknown piece of lifeless matter and a one-cell organism sprang to life, and all forms of life on earth evolved, and eventually produced the final result—mankind—after which, evolution evidently stopped.

No sediment of this "soup" has ever been found. Although, some should remain in the ancient rocks or surfaces.

Is it believable that this piece of matter knew how to obtain nourishment, knew how to duplicate itself, and how to eliminate toxins caused by metabolism, and could move around, although no brain or arms or legs, or any other body organs existed. Without the ability to nourish and protect itself, that spark of life would have just expired.

With all the plants and animals in the waters (fresh and salt) every sea organism, from sponges and coral to giant squids and whales; every land animal from bacteria to elephants and giraffes, including mankind; and every creature with wings, including bats, penguins, and ostriches, which theorists presume took billions of years to evolve, and the intense searches all over the world for evidence, wouldn't at least one little part of one life form, and one part of another have been found—if they ever existed?

Although evolution theorists adamantly defend and promote their presumptions, there is not one single shred of evidence to prove their theory is correct.

Evolution theorists presume some elements by "blind random chance", "floated" down to earth from "somewhere" into a lifeless "soup" which, also, by "blind random chance" formed in a lifeless ocean, on a lifeless planet, in a lifeless solar system, possibly in a lifeless galaxy.

There are 106 known elements. When and where did they originate? How did these elements get in the "soup?" Theorists blandly presume and tell us that these elements "floated" down from "somewhere" to Earth. From where? How did they originate there?

Some unknown force caused some elements to move around among all the other elements until by "blind random chance" they eventually joined to each other and hung together.

Only some of these 106 elements are in protoplasm—the only source of life—plant and animal. How did some lifeless chemicals separate and form the exact formulas for the 20 amino acids in proteins which, with fats and carbohydrates, form protoplasm?

Evolution theorists do not explain how or why lifeless chemical elements formed a lifeless (pre-biotic) "soup." They just presume they were there in the oceans and remained together in spite of tides, storms or other upheavals. There are over a hundred amino acids, but only 20 are in a protein.

Some elements randomly joined while floating around in a "slime" or "pre-biotic soup" in the oceans and others separated and remained separated in the same "soup." These elements supposedly just "floated" down from "somewhere" and formed the 20 necessary amino acids which randomly joined in a spot (cell) too small to be seen without a microscope—leaving out all the others—and immediately formed a membrane to hold them together and protect and nourish them.

Theorists don't explain if the one-cell formed instantly or over time. Cells must be nourished constantly and toxins from metabolic processes be removed. Theorists offer no explanation of how these processes occurred before the cell evolved the necessary organs to perform these functions.

Is it believable that by "blind random chance" these organs would have developed instantly?

Theorists do not say what kind of cell was instantly formed. A cell is very complex, with many separate parts. It duplicates itself into identical "daughter cells". There are millions of different cells, performing entirely different functions. There are 200 entirely different cells in a human body.

Phases of mitosis (cell duplication)

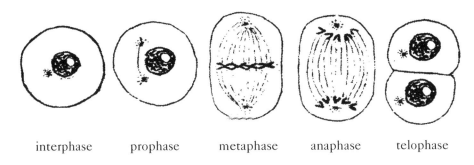

interphase　　prophase　　metaphase　　anaphase　　telophase

Evolution theorists tell us that by some unknown process, for some unknown reason, a one-cell organism suddenly sprang to life from lifeless matter, and for some unknown reason and by some unknown method decided to duplicate itself, and kept on duplicating itself, and in some way—they presume beneficial mutations—ignoring the harmful and fatal ones—evolved into all the life forms that have ever existed on Earth. That would take a lot of beneficial mutations, and even evolutionists accept the fact that for every beneficial mutation there are about a thousand or more harmful or lethal ones.

What unknown force caused this piece of lifeless matter to spring to life is not revealed by theorists. The how, why, when, and where criteria has not been met.

Is it believable that on a lifeless planet, in a lifeless "soup", that of the 106 known chemical elements, only four (carbon, hydrogen, nitrogen, oxygen) separated from all the others and somehow joined to form a one-cell organism, that somehow knew how to survive and reproduce, and by some unknown method evolved into every variety of creature that has ever inhabited the earth?

Another problem facing the evolution theory is that both sexes of a species had to evolve at the same time period and in the same area.

It has been asked, "What came first, the chicken or the egg?" Well, actually, it took two. If the rooster didn't fertilize the egg while it was in the hen's body before the shell formed, the egg would be infertile—no chicken, just a rotten egg.

Likewise, what came first, the plant or the seed? Well, actually it took two plants and usually a bee. And, they produced the same kind of plant. The presumption that a potato or a beet could evolve into a cabbage or tomato, or an apple or banana tree or a majestic redwood is utterly ridiculous. They have chromosomes too.

What came first, DNA or protein? It requires protein to form a cell. The DNA in a cell sends a message to the RNA to synthesize protein. The protein and the DNA had to be present at the cells beginning.

The knowledge of how to synthesize protein had to come from somewhere, and the protein, which with lipids and carbohydrates forms protoplasm—the basis of all living cells—had to be there at the same time. Evolutionists, theorists never explain this. They just presume it occurred.

DARWIN

Darwin's theory is the most accepted and quoted, so we shall challenge his theory based on modern medical knowledge and 21st Century research into how cells reproduce, how complex a cell is, recent discoveries in stem cell research, about hereditary genes, and how DNA in the nucleus of the cell determines what an organism will become.

Whether an organism becomes a man, an ape, a dog, or a cabbage is due to the number of chromosomes in the nucleus of the cells, which is determined at conception. Mankind has 46 chromosomes—23 pairs—half from the male parent and half from the female parent.

Charles Robert Darwin, an English Naturalist, lived from 1809 to 1882. He was admittedly a "rather below average scholar." He studied medicine at Edinburgh, studied Theology at Cambridge, but was not interested in becoming a clergyman. He was always interested in natural sciences and biology. As a boy he collected insects.

In December, 1831 Darwin, as naturalist, sailed from Davenport, England on HMS Beagle to complete a survey of South America and some Islands in that area.

At the beginning of his voyage on the Beagle, he apparently accepted the common belief in Creation.

It was during that voyage, which lasted for five years, that Darwin supposedly changed from the accepted belief of Creation to his presumptive theory of evolution—that all life had evolved from lifeless matter by "blind random chance" and a hit and miss process he called "natural selection" and "survival of the fittest."

Darwin: "I did not then in the least doubt the strict and literal truth of every word in the Bible."

Darwin: "Whilst on board the Beagle I was quite orthodox, and I remember being heartily laughed at by several of the officers (though themselves orthodox) for quoting the Bible."

Theorists presume that evolution happened slowly over millions of years. Picture a lifeless ocean on a lifeless planet. Try to picture how some chemical elements, in some unknown way, got into that lifeless ocean.

Then, by "blind random chance," by some unknown process, for some unknown reason, those elements joined to form a "soup," and those elements got to moving around and suddenly a one-cell organism sprang to life., and by some process, for some unknown reason started duplicating itself, although it had no brain or other intellectual processes.

Darwin never presumed to explain how the universe came to be, nor how our galaxy came to be, nor how the billions of other galaxies we can see, even without a telescope, came to be, how earth came to be, nor how gravity, which holds everything in place came to be.

He just starts with a lifeless earth, hanging somewhere in space.

Darwin had no evidence to support his evolution theory—not one shred of evidence of the transmutation of a single organism, and no such evidence has been discovered to date.

Darwin, nor any other scientist, has shown one shred of evidence of a cross-species. His examples show only varieties of a species, or improvements in a species.

Apparently during the stops in the Galapagos his observations into the many kinds of fauna, led him to his belief in the theory of evolution instead of Creation.

Darwin's first example of evolution were the 14 kinds of finches on the Gallapagos. In great detail he dwells on the differences in size, plumage, and beak formations. But his examples all involve finches, with bird's feet, wings, and feathers. He shows no examples of how a cold-blooded reptile became a warm-blooded bird. It was speculated scales became ragged and turned into feathers because the reptile was leaping around for prey. This ignored that a reptile changes skins several times a year.

In the Galapagos he observed the different appearance of finches, and labeled them different *species*, although these finches exhibited the same behavior and song pattern.

Darwin should have noticed they were still finches. They were not evolving into humming birds or field mice. There are still finches in many parts of the world.

But why his intense absorption with finches?

Darwin was an Englishman, traveling across the world. Did he not notice the difference in the human beings he encountered?

Did he not notice the difference in size, forms, features, colors, languages and habits? All races are the same species.

In Darwin's time, England and other parts of the world had cities, cultivation of crops, domestication of animals, books, music, cathedrals, factories, guns, but in other parts of the world humans were still uncivilized.

The American Indians were living in tents or caves, hunting for their food with bows and arrows, gathering available plants for food and medicine. Some even resorted to cannibalism. They wore skins and were wild and war-like.

Some tribes in other parts of the world were living in jungles. living in trees, or caves, and hunting for their food with spears, knives and clubs they made themselves. Some also practiced cannibalism.

Even after the Civil War Indians were living like that. Tribes in Africa were still living in the wild.

Eskimos' were living in igloos, hunting for their food with spears, and wearing skins.

These people used primitive tools, did not read or write, wore skins of animals. They all looked different in size, skin color. But they were all the same species—mankind.

All races of mankind, giants, pygmies, etc. are one species. They can interbreed, give blood transfusions, transplant organs, but not with animals (apes which we are supposed to be descendents of.) A monkey's heart was transplanted into a little girl and it was rejected. The child died.

It is very disturbing when Darwin speaks of "savages, Hottentots, and slaves."

Did he not realize that slaves were denied freedom, education, any chance whatsoever of improving their wretched existence?

Slavery was common in parts of the world in Darwin's time.

Charles Darwin was embarrassed by the fossil record—or lack thereof. Millions of bones (fossils) have been discovered by scientists, but not one shred of evidence has shown one part of one organism and one part of another.—none.

Surely of all the presumed evolution going on for millions of years, there would be a great number of fossils showing how one kind of life turns into another. No fossils have been found to support the evolution theory.

Darwin's theory of "natural selection," that is; the most fitted to the environment would survive, does nothing to explain how the most fitted came to be or how they became the fittest.

But Darwin had some doubts about his own theory as evidenced by the following quotes.

Darwin wrote to Asa Gray, a noted botanist of that era, "imagination must fill in the very wide gaps."

Darwin: "The distinctness of specific forms and their not being blended together by innumerable transitional links is a very obvious difficulty."

Darwin concedes "It is no doubt difficult even to conjecture by what transitions organs have arrived at their present state."

Darwin:

"There is another and allied difficulty which is much more serious. I allude to the manner in which species belonging to several of the main divisions of the animal kingdom suddenly appear in the lowest known fossiliferous rocks. The case at present must remain inexplicable, and may be truly urged as a valid argument against the views here entertained."

D: "The abrupt manner in which groups of species suddenly appear in certain formulation has been urged by several paleontologists . . . as a fatal objection to that belief in the transmutation of species,"

D: "To suppose that the eye could have been formed by evolution seems, I freely confess, absurd in the highest degree."

D: "Although the belief that an organ so perfect as the eye could have been formed by natural selection, is enough to stagger anyone."

———

D: "I look at the geological record as a history of the world imperfectly kept—imperfect to an extreme degree."

D: "To the question why we do not find rich fossiliferous deposits belonging to the earliest periods prior to the Cambrian system, I can give no satisfactory answer."

Darwin admitted an "infinitude of connecting links" was critical to his theory, but he was unable to demonstrate any existence of the missing connective links.

D: At the conclusion of the ORIGIN OF SPECIES concluded, "There is grandeur in this view of life, with its several powers, having been originally breathed by the Creator into a few forms or into one."

Added to Darwin's comments expressing some questions and comments regarding the fossil record, there are many dissenting views from noted scientists.

Colin Patterson (paleontologist, zoologist, evolutionist) "Speculation is free. But aside from such speculation it is generally accepted that the mutations supposedly involved in evolution are small accidental changes that accumulate over a long period of time."

Heribert Nilsson, a Swedish botanist, related after his research of 40 years, "It is not even possible to make a caricature of an evolution out of paleontological facts. The fossil material is now so complete that the lack of transitional series cannot be explained as due to the scarcity of material."

Christopher Booker, a British journalist, who believed in evolution, stated "We still have not the slightest demonstrable or even plausible idea of how evolution really took place . . . as to how it really happened we have not the slightest idea and probably never shall."

Robert Jastrow, astronomer: "Scientists have no proof that life was not the result of an act of creation."

Robert Jastrow:

"It is hard to accept the evidence of the human eye as a product of chance. It is even harder to accept the evolution of human intelligence as the product of random disruptions in the brain cells of our ancestors."

Jastrow "The critical first billion years, during which life began are blank pages in the Earth's history."

John D. Bernal (1901-1971) meteorologist, microbiologist, physicist, concluded, "We may never be able to explain it." There still is no explanation for "it" in the 21st Century.

Niles Eldridge, paleontologist, zoologist, "The pattern we were told to find for the last 120 years does not exist."

William Thorpe, Professor of Zoology at Cambridge,

"All the facile speculations and discussions published during the last ten or fifteen years explaining the mode of origin of life have been shown to be far too simple-minded and to bear very little weight. The problem in fact seems as far from solution as it ever was."

Darwin considered the change in plants and animals due to horticulture and husbandry, to be evolution.

Naturally, if the best plants or seeds are grown in an environment such as a greenhouse, with the best fertilizer and with proper watering for several generations, weeded and cultivated, they would improve over generations in that environment. Although change for the better—and some variants will occur,—a rose will still be a rose, and a cabbage will still be a cabbage.

If that garden is abandoned, you won't have better plants, you will have a weed patch.

If you are a dog breeder, and raise prize-winning show dogs; if you take pure-breed animals, and give them the best nutrients, grooming, and veterinary care, and rear them in a kennel, you might win prizes for best-of-breed. But turn that prize-winning dog out on the street, and you won't get a better breed, you will get curs.

This is what is called the "pendulum effect." It winds down not up.

The theory that all changes are an improvement is flawed, cultivation and domestication reveal that while some degree of change is possible, there are limits as to how far change can go.

Darwin was puzzled by finding similar plants and animals in various parts of the world. He believed they evolved in that location.

Did Darwin not know man is a nomad. He had to move on when food became scarce, or the environment changed drastically. He did no farming nor tamed animals for food.

Historians tell us Eskimos' and Indians crossed over to America on a land bridge from Asia to Alaska. How far could humans and animals travel in the millions of years evolution was supposed to occur? Man, animals, and birds could easily carry plants, and seeds during migration.

Of course, all plants and all animals have some related structures. Every plant and every animal is composed of the same thing—protoplasm.

Whether a man, an ape, a dog or a cabbage, everything is composed of protoplasm. What is protoplasm composed of? Lipids (fats), carbohydrates (starches and sugars) and proteins.

Plant life supposedly started in the ocean—algae. Where did algae come from? Is it believable that a plant, growing in water, could be tossed up on the shore, by "blind random chance," take root and grow?

Roots absorb water and minerals which is carried in the sap. Some trees are over a hundred feet tall, but this sap travels up the trunk to reach the leaves, etc. Root pressure starts the process, then water molecules take over. As water evaporates from the leaves it is recycled into the air to become rain.

Leaves get energy from the sun, carbon dioxide from the air, and water from the ground, and give off oxygen by a process called photosynthesis. This process occurs in cells so small a half-million could fit on the head of a pin. Photosynthesis involves about 70 elements—How they all came together by "blind random chance" is a miracle.

Scientists do not understand this process of photosynthesis and have been unable to duplicate it,

The Fossil Record—
Science or Fantasy?

What are fossils?

Fossils are skeletons or parts of skeletons such as skulls, jaw bones, a few teeth. They can also be shells, parts of wings or just an imprint or sediment in ancient rocks. They are the only records of the ancient past.

Examination of fossils supposedly supporting the evolution theory fail to do so.

If such fossils ever were, what happened to them?

The problem is they do not show a complete record. The only fossils found have been bits and pieces such as jaws, skulls, and teeth, not one complete skeleton from the most ancient creatures has been found. There is no skin, hair, features, soft tissues or organs. All these have been added by the artists' imagination and guesswork. The fossil record has been completely distorted to fit the presumptuous theory that all life has evolved from lifeless matter in a lifeless "soup" from a combination of lifeless elements.

Darwin was embarrassed by the fossil record because it did not support his theory of evolution. He attempted to explain this failure by stating "I look at the geological record as a history of the world imperfectly kept—imperfect to an extreme degree."

Surely, of all the presumed evolutionary processes involved in the billions of organisms, over millions of years, there would be many of such transitional forms, or parts of some transitional forms. There are millions of fossils recovered from all over the world, now available to scientific study and still not one—not a single transition or part of a transition—has been found

But, you ask, what about all the pictures of an ape-man? No evidence whatsoever has been discovered that such a creature ever existed. Drawings of so-called ape men are of the artists' guess work and invention.

Some evolutionists have promoted their theories with only these partial relics available. They add their imaginations and guesswork. They rely on and add on and some have distorted the evidence to support their evolution theory.

Darwin considered evolution to be a slow process, taking place over a vast time span. He presumed that evolution resulted when only beneficial mutations occurred to organisms, and the organism was able to decide which mutation would be beneficial to their descendents, and passed on only those mutations, avoiding all the harmful or lethal ones.

If so, there should be many fossils of transitional forms and stages, considering how many species of plants and animals there are.

Take for instance the "Peking Man." The entire representation of a stooped, hairy, ape-like man was from a skull, and jaw bones, no evidence of hair or posture.

For 43 years he was depicted as our ancestor but later, further inspection revealed it had been constructed from a human skull and the jaw bone of an ape and artificially aged.

Plants have revealed the same record—no transition forms from one plant to another—none.

Supposedly all plant life evolved from algae in the sea. How did the algae originate there is not addressed by theorists.

But plant life and animal life had to exist in the same time span.

Darwin cited the mistletoe as an example of evolution. He stated "mistletoe has seeds that must be transported by certain birds. It has flowers with separate sexes, absolutely requiring the agency of certain insects to bring pollen from one flower to the other."

Isn't it fortunate—but is it believable—that over millions of years of evolution, that both sexes of those certain trees, and those certain birds, those certain insects, and the already flowering mistletoe evolved in the same time span, in the same season, within the same location, just a few feet from each other.

Mistletoe doesn't grow every where.

Mutations—Beneficial or Harmful?

The evolution theory is based on the presumption that mutations have been the cause of the change from a one-cell organism into every species that has ever existed on Earth.

Evolutionists presume beneficial mutations have caused all the changes from a one-cell organism which evolved into all the animals, including mankind, and that an algae of some kind, from somewhere, evolved into all the plant life, just by "blind random chance," and hit and miss chances of inheriting some "acquired characteristics."

Theorists just ignore the possible results of any harmful mutations occurring at any phase of transmutations.

What are mutations? They are accidental changes in the genes in a cell.

Supposedly mutations are caused by a force such as lightning, excess sun, radiation, toxins, and by altered reproductive genes.

Scientists have experimented with altering genes, in fruit flies especially, and other animals. They have created no new species just freaks, such as arms or legs joined to abdomens, eyes in the wrong places and flies with four wings. A fly with four wings is still a fly.

How do mutations affect cellular activity? An example of that is a cancer—a malignant growth. A cell is altered by excess sun, radiation, toxins or whatever, and starts to grow and destroy normal cells.

Theodosius Dobzhansky (1900-1975) biologist said, "An accident, a random change in any delicate mechanism can hardly be expected to improve it."

The Encyclopedia America relates, "Because of the harmful nature of mutations, the fact that most mutations are damaging to the organism, seems hard to reconcile with the view that mutation is the source for raw material for evolution." Indeed, mutants illustrated in biology and text books are a collection of freaks and monstrosities. Mutation seems to be a destructive process, not a constructive process. Furthermore, there is no evidence to date supporting the evolution theory. No record of any mutation: whatever of any life form—plant or animal—changing in to another species.

Scientists have estimated, and presumably demonstrated, that the number of beneficial mutations to harmful ones is about a thousand lethal mutations to one beneficial one.

That seems a very shaky foundation to explain all the wondrous completely different life forms that have ever existed on Earth.

For evolution to be validated it is necessary to prove that every mutation would be beneficial and be passed on to future generations, over a very long time span.

Did all of the beneficial mutations occur to the same organism or did they spread out on innumerable off-springs in all directions; sea creatures—land animals—plants, each having vastly different structures?

How many beneficial mutations would any organism—the same organism—require to evolve from a worm to a human being?

How many times would a beneficial mutation—no harmful ones—affect the same organism? How many different kinds of mutations would have to occur during that organism's life span?

How many mutations could one organism stand with no damage, and how fortunate that if a leg for instance evolved—by many mutations—and, if it were a right leg, a mirror image left leg evolved at the same time. A fish with one leg and one fin wouldn't get very far. And after it managed to climb up on the shore, how long could it lie there panting before it evolved a right and left lung; a right and left arm; a right and left kidney; a right and left hemisphere in its brain, etc. The message is clear—not by "blind random chance."

How many beneficial mutations occurred to change a fish species to an amphibian species? How many fish and amphibians were involved? How many generations? Darwin perceived it was a very slow process.

Consider how many mutations a one-cell organism would go through to become all the sea creatures in the ocean, and how many mutations to become a land animal, a land vertebrate, and wind up as human?

If a one-cell organism did spring to life and knew how to duplicate itself, How long before another beneficial mutation occurred?

How long did these organisms live?

How many organisms would mutate a favorable feature—only one, or all of them at the same time? How many times would that organism duplicate itself and would the favorable mutation be inherited by any of the off-spring or some of them, or all of them? Would the same organism that did receive the favorable mutation inherit the next favorable mutation?

Then, did that descendent receive the next favorable mutation, or one that was harmful or lethal? Or might it be sterile, and evolution had to start over? It might or might not pass on the mutation—not all features are from one sex. How did both sexes evolve in the same time period, in the same place?

If an organism multiplied and another favorable mutation occurred to that same organism, would the mutations be passed on to all its descendants?

Can acquired characteristics be inherited? In the early 20th Century the conception that acquired characteristics could be inherited was widely rejected. The new studies of DNA had been discovered.

What process of evolution produced the genetic code, which modern scientists know, is what determines what an organism will be at the time of conception

Encyclopedia America states "reproduction of the DNA chain comprising a gene is remarkably accurate. Misprints or miscopying are infrequent accidents." Some evolutionists acknowledge beneficial mutations are few and infrequent. Think of all the billions of different species there are in the world and how many mutations had to occur to change each and every one,—one part at a time.

To how many organisms did the same mutation occur in the same part of the body? To all? If one wing evolved, did the other wing mutate into a matching pair? If not, what happened to a bird with part feathers and part scales? What are the possibilities the same bird would mutate a beak and bird claws and feathers and a song pattern? Birds supposedly evolved from reptiles.

If only beneficial mutations occurred, and an organism passed on those beneficial mutations, avoiding all harmful or lethal mutations, and after billions of evolutionary changes one species changed into a completely different species, i.e., a fish to an amphibian; an amphibian to a reptile; a reptile to a bird or mammal; where are all the millions of fossils, all over the world? There should be millions, maybe billions of fossils showing some sign of evolution—one part of one animal to a part of another. Not one has ever been discovered to date.

Did a fish, by some unknown incredible method, know how to become a land animal. How many fish were involved? How many had mutations? How many generations were involved? How long did each fish live? Are all acquired characteristics inherited, or only some? If a small thin man works his whole life doing body building exercises, eats to grow stronger, and winds up a muscle man, will his children inherit his muscles? Modern science believes they will not.

But, just suppose a fish started to grow a leg in place of a fin. Wouldn't that leg start as a few cells? It would have to be several different kinds of cells, all coming together by "blind random chance"—just the right kind of cells—skin, bone, red and white blood cells, muscle cells, nerve cells, etc, And wouldn't those cells divide and keep dividing to become a kind of knobby appendage—that no fish would recognize as something to help it survive—and by "natural selection", a right and left leg, arm, lung, kidney, eye, even a right and left hemisphere in the brain evolved? Is it believable that all these organisms received only the beneficial mutations—in sufficient numbers—and escaped all the harmful and lethal ones completely, and thus changed one species into another by "blind random chance"?

And, if by some reason, this knobby protrusion finally developed toes, ankles, knees, and hip joints, isn't it fortunate that the fish, "by blind random chance," grew a mirror-image leg on the other side of its body? And, if it finally crawled up on the shore, how long did it lie there panting until its gills evolved into lungs?

How many more mutations and how much time must occur before it became a useful leg? By what miracle did a mirror-image leg develop on the opposite side? One leg and one fin would not be beneficial. What about a right and left arm, right and left lungs, kidneys, eyes, ears, etc?

Did both right and left parts evolve at the same time? Miraculous?

For a one-cell organism that suddenly sprang to life from a piece of lifeless matter into a functioning organism it would take more than one blast of some force. One-cell organisms have more than one part. There are still one-cell organisms in existence today. They have to have body processes to eat and digest food, to breathe, and reproduce. Some one-cell organisms have both sex reproductive organs, but they exchange sperm with other like-organisms.

Plants had to follow the same path. Plants also have two different sexes. Plant and animal cells are very similar, are from the same material—protoplasm—and are very complex, with many separate and different parts.

And, at the same time sea algae, wherever it came from, evolved into all the plant life in the sea and all the plant life on earth. Plants take in carbon dioxide, and by a process called photosynthesis, emit the oxygen animal life needs to breathe, and at the same time animals breathe out the carbon dioxide plants need to live. Scientists admit they do not know how photosynthesis occurs, and have been unable to duplicate the process.

How remarkable that "blind random chance" could establish this very complex two-way process.

THE "SOUP"

Evolution theorists presume that all life on Earth originated in a pre-biotic "soup" or "slime" when an unknown force struck some unknown lifeless matter and that unknown matter suddenly sprang to life and not only knew how to obtain nourishment, eliminate toxins, but had to be able to move about, although it had no means to do so; and also knew how to duplicate itself. This is difficult to presume since that organism had not yet evolved a brain.

Evolutionists make no effort to explain where the "soup" came from or the unknown force—some speculate it was lightning—even though lightning usually destroys what it strikes. UV rays are also destructive, as is radiation.

Theorists presume the "soup" formed in an ocean. Which ocean? Or did it form in more than one? Where on planet Earth? Not in an extremely hot or extremely cold area. They presume the elements—over a hundred known—"floated" down to Earth from "somewhere."

How did they get "somewhere?" How, why, when, and where did they originate? How did they happen to join in exact, very complex formulas?

The chemical formula for water is H^2O—(2 parts hydrogen to 1 part oxygen.) There had to be water to form the soup. So the exact, formula for water, then—as it is today—just by "blind random chance" originated.

A small difference and water might not have formed, or been toxic. The atmosphere surrounding earth is 78% nitrogen, 21% oxygen and 1% carbon dioxide and other gases. A slight difference and it might be toxic to all life forms—plant and animal.

What did the presumed "soup" contain that made it possible for life to suddenly spring forth—presumably as a one-cell organism,— from which all life forms that ever existed on earth evolved.

There had to be atoms. Everything is composed of atoms— humans, animals, plants, cars, furniture—everything. The difference in objects and organisms is determined by the number of atoms and the number of neutrons and protons and the number and arrangement of the electrons in the atoms revolving around the nucleus, Scientists have discovered how to make bombs, one of which is powerful enough to destroy a city, but have no idea of what holds atoms together.

And, there had to be, the elements. There are 106 known elements, which evolutionists *presume* "floated" down from "somewhere", but where "somewhere" is and how over 100 elements originated there is not addressed.

How many of the elements "floated" in to the "soup?" Some of the elements are water soluble. Some are not.

Elements: exact formulas:

actinium—Ac
aluminum—Al
americium—Am
antimony—Sb
argon—Ar
arsemic—As
astatine—At
barium—Ba
berketrium—Bk
berre;;ium—Be
bismuth—Bi
boron—B
bromine—Br
cadmium—Cd
calcium Ca
californium—Cf
carbon—C
cerium—Cr
cesium—Cs
chlorine—Cl

chromium—Cr
cobalt—Co
copper—Cu
curium—Cm
dysprosium—Dy
einsteinium—Es
element 106
erbium—Er
europium—Eu
fermium—Fm
fluorine—F
francium—Fr
gadolinium—Gd
gallium—Ga
germanium—Ge
gold—Au
Hafnium—Hf
helium—He
hahnium—Ha
helium—He

holmium—Ho
hydrogen—H
indium—In
iodine—I
iridium—Ir
iron—Fe
krypton—Kr
lanthanum—La
lawrencium—Lr
lead—Pb
lithium—Li
lutetium—Lu
magnesium—Mg
manganese—Mn
mendelevium—Md
mercury—Hg
molybedenum—Mo
neodumium—Nd
neon—Ne
neptunium—Np
nickel—Ni
niobium—Nb
nitrogen—N
nobelium—No
osmium—Os
oxygen O
palladium—Pd
phosphorus—P
platinum—Pt
plutonium—Pu
polonium—Po
potassium—K
praseodymium—Pr

promethium—Pm
protactinium—Pa
radium Ra
radon—Rn
rhenium—Re
rhodium—Rh
rubidium—Rb
ruthenium—Ru
rutherfordium Rf
samarium—Sm
scandium—Sc
selenium—Se
silicon—Si
silver—Ag
sodium—Na
strontium—Sr
sulfur—S
tantalum—Ta
technetium—Tc
tellurium—Te
terbium—Tb
thallium—Tl
tin—Sn
titanium—Ti
tungsten—W
uranium—U
vanadium—V
xenon—Xe
Ytterbium—Yb
Yttrium—Y
Zinc—Zn
zirconium Zr

So how many and what proportion of these elements had to join, keeping all others out, to form the "matter" that was able to "spring to life."

What kind of lifeless matter sprang to life? It would have to be protoplasm.

PROTOPLASM:

The only known form of matter in which life is present. It is the essential material of all life—plants and animals. It is composed mainly of proteins, lipids (fats), and carbohydrates (starches and sugars), and inorganic salts.

Protoplasm could not be present in a pre-biotic "soup" without proteins which is a very complex combination of amino acids.

AMINO ACIDS:

There are hundreds of amino acids but twenty had to separate and join together in the presumed "soup," along with fats and carbohydrates. Evolutionists make no effort to explain where all these formulas originated or why, how or when.

There are 106 known elements, but only four (C, H, N, O) are present in amino acids.

Amino acids are not just specks of some kind of matter.

Amino acids are exact formulas which supposedly joined together by "blind random chance" in the lifeless "soup," and remained together, keeping all other elements out, although the soup was moving (stirring) by wind, tides, and currents in an ocean.

Amino acids are the basic structural unit of proteins.

THE 20 AMINO ACIDS ESSENTIAL TO FORM A PROTEIN:

alamine	$C_3H_7NO^2_2$
arginine	$C_6H_{14}N_4O_2$
asparagine	$C_4H_8N_2O_3$
aspartic acid	$C_4H_7NO_4$
cysteine	$C_3H_7NO_2S$
glutamic acid	$C_5H_9NO_4$
glutamine	$C_5H_{10}N_2O_3$
glycine	$C_2H_5NO_2$
histidine	$C_6H_9N_3O_2$
isoleucine	$C_6H_{13}NO_2$
leucine	$C_6H_{13}NO_2$
lysine	$C_6H_{14}N_2O_2$

methionine .... $C_5H_{11}NO_2S$
phenylalanine .... $C_9H_{11}NO_2$
proline .... $C_5H_9O_2N$
serine .... $C_3H_7NO_3$
threonine .... $C_4H_9NO_3$
tryptophan .... $C_{11}H_{12}N_2O_2$
tyrosine .... $C_9H_{13}NO^3$
valine .... $C_5H_{11}NO^2$

PROTEIN:

Essential base for all life—plant and animal.

There are many kinds of proteins which perform many different functions. Protein is formed of oxygen, usually sulfur, and occasionally other elements such as iodine, iron, and phosphorus, etc.

Protein includes other essential compounds such as enzymes, hormones and immunoglobins. Protein is in the structural material in muscles, tissues, and organs, and regulates the functions of hormones and enzymes, and forms glucose which is used as an energy source.

There are about 2000 protein enzymes required for cellular activity.

How likely, by "blind random chance," would these exact formulas and combinations of exact formulas, combine in a lifeless "soup," to form the proteins essential in all life—plants and animals?

If only one amino acid formula is altered in a protein sequence, it will change the proteins ability to function which affects red blood cells so they cannot properly carry nutrients and oxygen to all the body parts.

CELLS

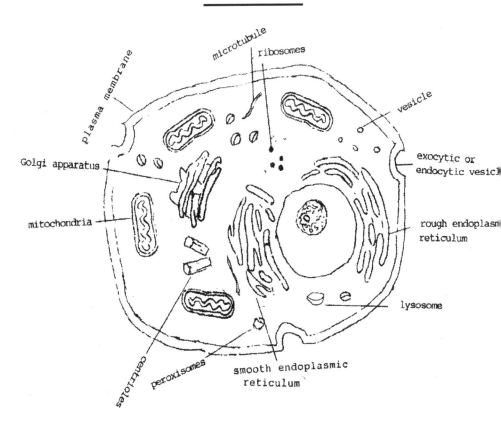

Because both our education and training is in the medical field, we will use the human cells as examples.

The main parts of the cell are cytoplasm and nucleus. Cytoplasm makes up the body mass—which becomes tissue. The nucleus controls activities of cells—helps cells divide.

Cytoplasm contains mitochondria which supplies most of the cell's energy. The nucleus controls growth, repair, and reproduction. The nucleus contains one or more nucleolus (nucleolei). The nucleolus' major role is protein synthesis. It is composed of ribonucleic acid (RNA)

The human body is made up of two main type of cells, somatic and gonadal. Somatic cells (body cells) become tissues, organs, and systems. Gonadal cells (spermatocytes and oocytes) unite to produce a new individual.

Somatic cells replicate themselves by mitosis—a precise process of division which produces two identical "daughter cells."

Gonadal cells (gametes) divide by meiosis. Instead of doubling as in mitosis, the gonadal cells are halved (haploid process). When an ovum is fertilized the original number of chromosomes is restored from the other parent.

A fertilized ovum divides into masses of new cells by mitosis. Groups of cells develop similarities, and these cells, together with their membrane (plasmalemma), form a tissue.

Deoxyribonucleic acid (DNA) is the heredity gene in every cell. It duplicates itself and passes on exact copies of the genetic code to future generations.

PARTS OF CELLS

CENTRIOLE: (pair) involved in the formation of the spindle and aster during cell division.

CHROMATIN: consists of DNA and protein, condensed into chromosomes during mitosis and meiosis.

CYTOPLASM: codes genetic information in the DNA and RNA chains, surrounds the nucleus of a cell.

CYTOSKELETON: active in cell movement.

ENDOPLASMIC RETICULUM: transports materials within cells. where proteins and lipids are formed. Smooth and rough.

GOLGI COMPLEX APPARATUS: involved in modification and transport of proteins

LIPOSOME: organelle containing various enzymes.

MICROTUBULE: component of the cytoskeleton, cilia, and flagella.

MICROVILLI: microscopic projection of a cell, organelle or tissue.

MITROCHONDRIA: produces energy for the cell.

NUCLEOLUS: contains RNA for ribosome and protein synthesis.

NUCLEUS: organelles to cell function as protein synthesis and reproduction. Contains the DNA and RNA.

PEROXISOME: organelle containing enzymes for production and decomposition of hydrogen peroxide.

RIBOSOMES: any RNA and protein or cytoplasmic organelles that are areas of protein synthesis.

VACUOLE: a cavity vesicle in the cytoplasm of a cell, contains fluid. White blood cells form vacuoles when they surround and digest bacteria or other foreign matter.

VESICLE: fluid-filled pouch in the cells of plants and animals.

CELL: A small, usually microscopic, mass of protoplasm, forming the smallest structural unit of living matter capable of functioning independently. A cell is bounded externally by a semi permeable membrane, usually containing one or more nuclei,

Cells, alone, or interacting with other cells, perform all the fundamental functions of life.

Cells are the basic units of all living matter—plant and animal. They are different shapes, sizes, and perform many different functions.

There are 200 completely different cells in the human body The human brain contains billions of cells (neurons)

Nerve cells send signals along axons.

White blood cells have flexible membranes which can pass through spaces between capillaries.

Muscle cells' lengths can vary to change contractural force.

Sperm cells have whip-like tails to propel them through the female genital tract to fertilize the ovum.

Female eggs (ova) develop a membrane after fertilization to prevent any more sperm from entering.

Which of these cells evolved into another? And, there are many more kinds of cells to consider.

Evolutionists tell us that for some unknown reason a cell, by some unknown process, sprang to life from lifeless matter, and had the knowledge of how to survive, and how to reproduce itself. They never say how this process originated nor where the knowledge came from, nor where the lifeless matter and unknown force came from.

Scientists now know cells reproduce only identical (daughter) cells.

What kind of cell sprang to life and knew how to duplicate itself? Cells don't just duplicate themselves. They go through phases. This process is called cytokinesis.

A skin cell would produce a skin cell; a blood cell would produce a blood cell; a lung cell would produce a lung cell.

MITOSIS: The cell duplication phases.

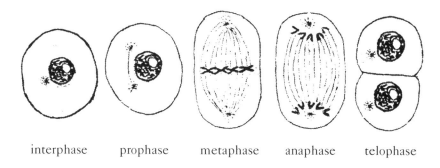

interphase   prophase   metaphase   anaphase   telophase

Theorists also tell us these amazing cells knew what mutations were beneficial, and knew how to avoid all harmful or lethal mutations, although scientific research shows that harmful mutations happen thousands to a few beneficial ones. These beneficial mutations were retained and passed on to future generations over a vast time span.

They still do not explain how this cell processed all this knowledge, as it had not yet evolved a brain.

Then this one cell—by only beneficial mutations—kept evolving and changing species into all the creatures in the ocean, from sponges and coral to giant squids and whales; all the animals on earth from bacteria to elephants and giraffes; and everything with wings, including ostriches, penguins, and bats. They presume all this occurred by "blind random chance" and a hit and miss process Darwin called 'natural selection" and "survival of the fittest."

Is it believable that all these different cells evolved from lifeless matter? That some, performing the same functions, formed into tissues, and that the tissues formed into different organs; that the organs united and formed different systems; and all these systems— although functioning independently—formed together to become a body. All systems perform independently, but anything affecting one, affects the entire body.

Is it believable that by "blind random chance", these cells, tissues, and organs all reached the proper area in the body, and knew how to perform with each other to support the life of the body?

Since cells duplicate themselves, producing identical cells, there could be no way to transform any one cell in to the 200 different cells in the human body,

All body processes take place at the cellular level as a result of metabolic action.

All cells need a constant supply of nutrients and oxygen and the constant removal of toxins from the metabolic process. The nutrients are carried to each individual cell by red blood cells, and toxins are carried away If the supply of blood is interrupted the organ dies,

Billions of brain cells (neurons) are present at birth, and are never replaced.

All body cells are replaced regularly. It is estimated that all the body cells are replaced every seven years.

Although cells have been examined for many years, in the 21st Century better microscopes have enabled scientists to further study the very complex cell.

Darwin apparently had no knowledge of how complex a cell is, no knowledge of the genetic code by which organisms are formed.

Darwin presumed that "blind random chance" was the source for every change in all creatures.

Recent knowledge about heredity and how the genetic code affects each of us and how it is passed on to future generations contradicts the theory that "blind random chance" determines what kind of organism will evolve, or that "natural selection", or "survival of the fittest" results in a different species.

All 21st Century Scientific research on stem cells, artificial insemination, cloning, etc. is done using live cells. No scientist or anyone else has been able to produce a speck of life from lifeless matter.

Louis Pasteur, after many years of study and experiments, concluded, "Life comes only from previous life."

Blood is made up of billions of cells. It circulates through the body in plasma. Plasma is the liquid part of blood—about 90%.

A drop of blood contains approximately 5 million red blood cells.

Blood cells are very small. About 50 or 60 thousand would fit in a space as small as the head of a pin.

Blood contains proteins, sugars, fats, vitamins, hormones, and minerals such as calcium, magnesium, sodium, etc., and gases such as oxygen, carbon dioxide, etc, and waste products (such as uric acid, urea, etc.,) from metabolic processes.

The heartbeat carries the blood and the brain regulates the heartbeat, and breathing. No oxygen or blood supply, the heart and brain dies. The *entire* body parts must work together. Evolving one part at a time would never support life.

Erythrocytes (red blood cells) form in the long bones (arms, legs, ribs, etc.)

Erythrocytes survive about four months. Millions die off each minute but are quickly replaced.

Red blood cells carry nutrients and oxygen to every cell in the body

If blood does not reach a part of the body, that part dies.

White blood cells defend against infections and bacteria. They engulf and destroy bacteria by a process called phagocytosis

After an acute stage of infection, eosinophils clear up dead tissues and bacteria.

It is estimated there are possibly 30 to 40 billion white blood cells in the human body,

Platelets control clotting.

The DNA contained within each cell holds specific information (the genetic code) which will be passed on to future generations, as well as for protein synthesis. It takes protein to form DNA and DNA information to form protein. So, which evolved first?

Atoms in DNA form a spiral, which can only be observed through a microscope, but if unwound could measure up to 5 feet in length.

CELL MEMBRANE:

At the same time the cell evolved, the cell membrane (plasmalemma) had to evolve.

The plasma membrane surrounds the cell and encloses cytoplasm and the cell nucleus. The plasma membrane separates metabolic internal processes from outside environmental processes and selectively allows some substances to enter the cells, and keeps other substances out. The plasmalemma is complex. It is a double lipid bilayer (phospholipid) membrane.

The plasma membrane is a semi permeable limiting layer of cell protoplasm consisting of three layers. The inner and outer layers are composed of protein and the middle layer is composed of a double layer of fat molecules.

The presumptuous theory that all life evolved from a one-cell organism contradicts everything presently known about cell formation and duplication.

Human life does begin in one cell, but not a one-cell organism. The single cell is a zygote (a fertilized ovum). That single cell has many parts. The nucleus contains the DNA, which does determine what the organism will be. When a male and female unite, at conception the genetic code determines what we are to be and our physical appearance, and what is passed on to future generations.

MANKIND

PREHISTORIC TO MODERN

anthropology—study of human culture

archeology—study of ancient relics

paleoanthropology—study of prehistoric remains

paleontology—study of fossils

Darwin and other evolutionists have adamantly persisted in their claims that humans have evolved from a single-cell organism, with apes as our ancestors.

No evidence of any presumed evolution has been discovered. Darwin was aware of this problem. He stated in a letter to Asa Gray, a botanist, "imagination must fill in the very wide gaps."

A century and a half later, the "gaps," commonly known as the "missing links." are still missing. None of Darwin's theory has been validated by actual evidence of a single discovery of a cross species, or parts of a cross species, since he wrote ORIGIN OF SPECIES.

Nor have 21st Century scientists found an answer in the oldest rocks. There are no fossils showing gradual changes of ancient forms, and no sediment of a "soup" or "slime."

There remains a total absence of transitional fossils or parts of fossils.

The fossil record, which is the only record of the history of the ancient world, has been interpreted by evolutionists with great imagination and guesswork, from a few bits and pieces of skeletal remains. But what, you may ask, of all the pictures of "ape-men" shown in all the scientific journals and textbooks"?

In evaluating the evidence of a presumed evolution, it is necessary to realize that the drawings of an "ape-man" are based on bits and pieces of bones. There have been no hair, skin, soft tissues, organs, or features, available of those ancient creatures.

Modern technology has shown some of the supposed fossils to be fakes, and drawings of others to be only the result of the artist's imagination and artistic ability.

With no more fossils than teeth and jaw bones it isn't possible to know what the creatures looked like, but the "educated guessing" and speculation of the rest of the organism is a sample of how the evolutionists filled in the blanks to promote their theory.

There have been several ancient species which at some period were presumed to be the ancestors of mankind. Most were later acknowledged to be non-human.

The best known supposed fossil of a part-ape, part-man is the Piltdown man, referred to as the Peking man. The drawing was made from only a jaw and skull.

For about 43 years it was accepted by scientists as the "missing link,", but in 1953 it was exposed as a hoax when it was exposed that parts of a human skull and parts of an orangutan's jaw and teeth were put together and artificially aged.

Parts of a woman (the scientists who discovered it named Lucy) was estimated to have lived about 3 million years ago. She was small, about the size of a four or five year old child today. Her age was presumed to be about 25 years old when she died.

Scientists made these estimations although they did not find all of her skeleton.

Although "Lucy" was very small There is no evidence that all who lived at that time were also that small. Males could have been larger. Also, we have dwarfs born of normal-size parents, and who have normal-size children to date.

RAMAPITHECUS: 14 million years ago

Reconstructed from only teeth and upper and lower jaw bones, was originally called the link between mankind and apes, but, more recent and complete fossil finds showed the Ramathecus to be more similar to a modern ape than to a man.

AUSTRALOPITHECUS: 3 to 4 million years ago

Research into ancient fossils of the Australopithecus showed that their skull was very different from humans, and much more similar to apes.

HOMO ERECTUS:

The brain size and shape were dissimilar to humans, although the arms and leg bones were similar.

HOMO HABILIS: 1.5 to 2.5 million years ago were the first people scientists can agree were our direct ancestors. They made and used tools, they lived in small huts. They had larger brains. They made more complex tools. Used fire.

HOMO SAPIENS:

Homo sapiens appeared about 150,000 years ago, known as the Neanderthals

NEANDERTHALS:

The Neanderthals were named for the region in France where many remains were discovered.

The first Neanderthal remains found were believed to be of a stooped, hairy, ape-man. Later fossils show that the first remains were of a man deformed by disease, possibly rickets.

Later fossils show the Neanderthals as being not much different than modern mankind and in some ways superior.

A Neanderthal man was about 5'5" or 5'6" in height, and powerfully built, with thick bones. He was agile and had manual dexterity. Some skeletons have been discovered with intact hyoid bones (voice boxes). The Neanderthals were capable of speech.

Their vertebrae were similar to modern mankind, showing strong arms and shoulders, and hands capable of grasping, pulling, and lifting. The lower limbs were straight and strong, in keeping with bipedal walking.

Their brains were larger than modern man's.

The Neanderthal lived in bands in caves. He utilized fire. He created and used tools. He painted pictures on cave walls.

Burial sights were found with remains of flower seeds, etc. Apparently he had a religion.

That isn't exactly the image of an ape man. It's more like the culture of the American Indian in Darwin's time.

CRO MAGNON:

The Cro Magnon lived about 40 thousand years ago. He was very much like modern humans. Remains found in Southern France showed he had a large brain, stood and walked erect. He produced tools from bone and flint. He lived in caves or huts, utilized fire for cooking and heating. He created jewelry. He did rock carving and painted pictures of people, animals and plants on rocks and cave walls. He carved sculptures and made jewelry. Some carved symbols might be considered the start of written language.

Apparently they practiced religion and cared for the helpless and elderly.

All races of mankind are the same species. They can give blood transfusions, organ transplants, and mate and have children.

HUMANITY

Here we are. How did we get here?

So far, modern scientists have been unable to contact any evidence of life anywhere else in the Universe by space travel, radio waves, or telescopic observations.

Does life exist anywhere else except on planet Earth?

Evolution theorists tell us that life began on Earth by "blind random chance" and a hit and miss process.

To consider humanity as the "fittest" is an odd conclusion. Humans are weaker than many of the larger species. They cannot run as fast. They have no body hair or fur to protect them from solar rays or the elements. They have to reach puberty (about 12 or 13 years of age) before they can reproduce. Females can conceive only during their ovulation period—about three days each month for about 30 years.

And there is usually a single birth after about a nine-month gestation period. Human infants are completely helpless for years. They require constant care. It sounds revolting, but human infants would lie in their own feces and vomit in their own faces if not cared for. They cannot crawl for months nor walk for about a year.

Yet, this strange species is the predominant species over the entire world.

The human body is a miracle. If it is cut, it immediately begins to repair the damage. If a disease attacks it immediately starts to fight the infection.

The brain interprets sight and hearing just from vibrations and light senses, and regulates breathing, blood pressure, body temperature, and heartbeat. What in the mutation process could perfect such a system?

So, if the human body is a miracle, what about the human brain? Millions of bits of information reach the brain through the senses and environment, and is processed and handled as to importance. The reticulum formation in the brain stem, a network of neurons (nerves) monitors and controls the millions of messages coming into the brain and allows only some of them to be acted on.

The billions of neurons in the brain are not connected. They are separated by spaces called synopses, which are about a millionth of an inch across.

Some scientists have estimated there are billions of neurons in the human brain and every neuron has perhaps a quadrillion connections.

Is it believable that anything as awesome as the human brain evolved by "blind random chance" from lifeless matter?

A computer is not an electric brain as some have described. It took a brain to formulate a computer

Carl Sagan, a U.S. astronomer, estimated that the brain could contain enough information that "would fill some twenty million volumes, as many as the world's largest libraries."

How the brain produces thoughts has never been explained, but abstract thinking, such as visualizing the use for a wheel, and fire, to the concepts of space travel, and the internet, television, and cell phones is truly awesome.

Consider colored television; traveling through space; consider cell phones. We talk to each other daily from California to Missouri—no wires. If one of us travels to Colorado and the other to Hawaii, we can still talk to each other by calling the same numbers, and just holding a cell phone to our ears. How did that abstract thinking that envisioned such wonderful things—let alone invent them—happen? No one has explained by what method such abstract thinking evolved from lifeless matter.

The brains of humans compose symphonies, paint masterpieces, write novels, reads, writes, and speaks. Humans hang lace curtains, cook gourmet meals, use fire, and utilized the wheel. They invented the internet and television, travel the world via jet planes, travel through space, drive along the freeways talking on cell phones that can take and store pictures, map directions, take messages and access the internet.

Visit a farm. Go on safari. What are those animals doing?

You can take an infant from the most savage, uncivilized tribe, adopt the child into a modern civilized home, rear it in a modern culture, educate it in a good university, and when that child is an adult it can become a doctor, lawyer, scientist, or a computer genius. All the intelligence and capabilities are already there. No evolution needed—just opportunity.

Isolation, environment and culture have more effect on mankind than a presumed evolution.

In summary, we believe we must admit the amazing brain of man has yet to understand the beginning of life and the infinity of time and space. Man is limited to what he can see, taste, hear, sense, smell and touch. There may be a sixth sense (ESP), but it cannot be observed or demonstrated. So should we just admit we do not know how, why, where or when life originated?

Albert Einstein said he did 'try humbly to comprehend even an infinitesimal part of the intelligence manifest in nature"

CONCLUSION

Each species is determined by a genetic code, located in the nucleus of its cells. Each species has a different code. The human body has 46 chromosomes—half of each pair is from the maternal parent and half from the paternal parent, joined at conception If one of these pairs triples for some unknown reason, it does not produce a new species. The result is a child with Down's syndrome.

A human does develop from a single cell. But it's not a cell that suddenly sprang to life from lifeless matter. That cell is a zygote.

A zygote is a fertilized ovum from a human female with the sperm from a human male. This cell holds the genetic code which dictates that it will become a human being. This genetic code is formed at conception.

Conception of humans requires a male after puberty and a female after puberty, and must occur during the female's ovulation period, which occurs once in her monthly cycle. The only exception is in laboratory conditions such as artificial insemination or cloning.

All stem cell research, artificial insemination and cloning is done on live cells, not lifeless "matter." No scientist has been able to produce one spark of life by any means whatsoever.

Both male and female humans have completely different reproductive systems. Billions of sperm is released at each ejaculation, but usually only one reaches an ovum, and most times not even one.

The ovum and sperm do not survive outside the human body, except in controlled laboratory conditions.

Fertilization must occur within the female body. This involves not only two completely different sets of sexual organs, but, also, emotional responses such as desire and stimulation.

If an ovum is fertilized and conception occurs, the first part of the fetus to develop is the brain and spinal cord.

Nothing works without the brain. The brain regulates body temperature, blood pressure, breathing, and everything else.

Eyes cannot see until the brain interprets the visual images.

The ears cannot hear until the vibrations entering the ear reach the brain and are interpreted.

The brain requires constant nutrition and oxygen, as do the other organs in the body. Red blood cells (erythrocytes) are formed in the long bones—arms, legs, ribs, etc), and are circulated to every cell in the body. If circulation is stopped and no blood and oxygen reach the heart or brain, that organ dies. The circulation is regulated by the beat of the heart, which is regulated by the brain. No part of the body exists without the other part. There are 10 different body systems, with different cells, tissues, and organs. Each system works independently, but what affects one, affects the entire body.

The brain is the first organ to develop in a fetus

When the brain shows a flat line on the monitor, life is ended.

The brain regulates all body processes—the heart beat, body temperature, blood pressure, breathing, etc.

Brain cells (neurons) require constant nutrients and oxygen and toxins from metabolic activity removed. This is carried out by the circulation system. Red blood cells carry oxygen and nutrition to every cell in the body.

The evolution theory is widely accepted, although to date, no scientists have been able to validate any part of the theory and no form or any other evidence of any life form changing to another life form, nor any part of one life form changing in to any other part of any organism has ever been discovered.

There are a trillion cells in a human body, 200 completely different cells. Cells are all shapes and sizes and perform different functions in different areas of the body.

Cells multiply by mitosis, a four-stage process that produces identical "daughter cells." A red blood cell does not become a different kind of cell.

Scientific experiments on fruit flies and other animals by altering genes, has not resulted in any new species. Such alterations have produced only freaks and monstrosities. They have produced fruit flies with two sets of wings; eyes and limbs of organisms in the wrong parts of bodies, but the fruit fly is still a fly and other animals remain the same species. No new species of any kind has been a result of such experiments.

Is it believable that by "blind random chance" and a hit and miss process Darwin called "natural selection" and "survival of the fittest," a miracle such as the human body, mind, and emotional capacity evolved from "lifeless matter." How did the yearning for such as art and music, religion, and abstract thinking of everything from the wheel to the internet evolve from nothing?

Is it possible to even imagine absolute NOTHING? Can we accept that everything in our world started from NOTHING?

Darwin wrote "imagination must fill in the very wide gaps." That takes a lot of imagination—but where did imagination originate?

The entire evolution theory is based on the presumption that all organisms could "select" which evolutionary changes would be beneficial to its descendents, and its "survival" skills. Wow! From what lifeless matter did that knowledge evolve?

In summary we believe we have to admit the amazing brain of man has yet to understand the beginning of life or the infinite.

So let us admit we do not know how life originated, nor where, nor why, nor when. Maybe someday we will.

For now, we must acknowledge there is a lot to learn.

THE EVOLUTION THEORY? HOW PRESUMPTUOUS!